DIANA

Queen of Hearts

BY MARC CERASINI

Random House 🏠 New York

To Prince William and Prince Harry

Cover photograph credits (front): Jayne Fincher/Gamma Liaison; (back): Express News/ Archive Photos

Insert photograph credits: CP/Globe Photos, p. 1 (top); CP/Globe Photos, p. 1 (middle); CP/Globe Photos, p. 1 (bottom); CP/Globe Photos, p. 2 (top); Express News/Archive Photos, p. 2 (bottom); Express News/Archive Photos, p. 3 (top); Photographers Int./Gamma Liaison, p. 3 (middle); Jim Bennett/CP/Globe Photos, p. 3 (bottom); Globe, p. 4 (top); Alpha/Globe Photos, p. 4 (middle); Gamma Press/Gamma Liaison, p. 4 (bottom); Reuters/R. Reagan Pres. Library/Archive Photos, p. 5 (top); Alpha/Globe Press, p. 5 (bottom); CP/Globe Photos, p. 6 (top); Patrick Demarchelier/CP/Globe Photos, p. 6 (bottom); Georges De Keerle/Gamma Liaison, p. 7 (top); De Keerle/Apesteguy/Gamma Liaison, p. 7 (bottom); Alpha/Globe Photos, p. 8 (top); Spooner/Gamma Liaison, p. 8 (bottom left); Spooner/Gamma Liaison, p. 8 (bottom right); PA News/Archive Photos, p. 9 (top); Reuters/Dominic Wong/Archive Photos, p. 9 (bottom); Jayne Fincher/Gamma Liaison, p. 10 (top); Reuters/Mike Segar/Archive Photos, p. 10 (bottom); Dave Chancellor/ Alpha/Globe Photos, p. 11 (top); Alpha/Globe Photos, p. 11 (bottom); Reuters/Jose Manuel/Archive Photos, p. 12 (top); Dave Chancellor/Alpha/Globe Photos, p. 12 (bottom); Reuters/J. M. Ribeiro/Archive Photos, p. 13 (top); Ashley Knotek/Alpha/Globe Photos, p. 13 (bottom); Dave Chancellor/Alpha/Globe Photos, p. 14 (top and bottom); Cisotti/ Deidda/Alpha/Globe Photos, p. 15 (top); Porter Gifford/Gamma Liaison, p. 15 (bottom); Snowdon/CP/Globe Photos, p. 16

The Pediatric AIDS Foundation is the leading national non-profit foundation identifying, funding, and conducting critical pediatric AIDS research worldwide. The foundation is working to find ways to prevent the transmission of AIDS from an HIV-infected pregnant woman to her newborn, to prolong and improve the lives of children with HIV, to eliminate HIV in infected children, and to promote education, awareness, and compassion about this disease.

For more information, please contact:
Pediatric AIDS Foundation
1311 Colorado Avenue
Santa Monica, Calif. 90404
(310) 395-9051 or for donations (888) 499-HOPE
http://www.PedAIDS.org

Once upon a time, not very long ago, a beautiful young woman married a handsome prince. He was the most eligible bachelor in the world. She—quite literally—was the girl next door.

While 750 million people in seventy-four countries all around the world watched in awe, Lady Diana Frances Spencer emerged from the crystal carriage that brought her to the entrance of St. Paul's Cathedral in London. Diana had come to say her vows to Charles, the Prince of Wales, and heir to the throne of England. On that July day in 1981, the shy, self-conscious girl next door would be transformed into the Princess of Wales.

She was only twenty years old, and the whirlwind courtship and lavish wedding ceremony seemed like a fairy tale come true.

The wedding itself was the largest and most splendid ceremony ever mounted in the history of the British monarchy. It was attended by presidents and princes, kings and queens, the rich and the powerful.

But as Diana walked down the aisle at St. Paul's, her bridal train streaming out behind her, she had doubts about the marriage she was entering into, doubts about her handsome prince's true feelings for her.

On that day, however, and in the days leading up to it, Diana felt powerless in the grip of titanic forces propelling her forward on the path to royalty. On her shoulders now rested the hopes and dreams of her country, the royal family, and her own family and friends, not to mention the expectations and excitement of people around the world.

As Diana vowed to love, honor, and cherish her prince forever, a voice deep inside told her that she would never become Queen of England.

But could she have somehow sensed, on that glorious day full of pomp and ceremony, that she would one day become the queen of all our hearts?

Chapter 1

"*Just*" *a Girl*

The Honourable Diana Frances Spencer arrived in the world late in the afternoon of July 1, 1961. She was the third daughter of aristocratic parents, thirty-seven-year-old Johnnie Spencer and twenty-five-year-old Frances Roche.

Unfortunately, Diana's birth was met with disappointment. Her father, who held the title Viscount of Althorp, dearly wanted a son to carry on the family name and tradition. He already had two daughters, four-year-old Sarah and eight-year-old Jane.

The parents had wanted a boy so much that they had not even considered any girls' names before Diana's birth. It was almost a week before they finally settled on the names "Diana Frances," after the girl's mother and a Spencer ancestor.

Diana's birth was made even more difficult for her parents because a son had been born to them just eighteen months before. But the infant, named John Spencer, was so sick that he lived for only ten hours. His passing had left the Spencers without a male heir. This was considered a serious situation for a noble family.

Once the richest sheep traders in Europe, the Spencers had a long and illustrious history. They received an earldom, or noble title, from King Charles I in the fifteenth century. With their growing wealth and prominence, the Spencer family built Althorp House in Northamptonshire. They acquired a family crest and the motto "God defend the right."

In the centuries that followed, members of the Spencer family held many important royal offices and positions of power in England and abroad. Diana, through her father, was related to King Charles II and the Duke of Marlborough. On her mother's side of the family, Diana was distantly related to seven American presidents, including Franklin Delano Roosevelt.

She was also distantly related to the popular American actor Humphrey Bogart, star of the movie *Casablanca*.

At the time Diana was born, the Spencer family was not as wealthy as it once had been. Still the Spencers possessed a significant fortune, an estate, and a huge collection of rare books and pieces of art.

But it was through her mother's family, the Fermoys, that the Spencers came to own Park House, Diana's cozy childhood home in Norfolk.

4

Park House was a wonderful place for a child to grow up. Surrounding it were horse stables, dog kennels, a heated swimming pool, and a beautiful estate that bordered on a huge wooded area.

This small estate where Diana lived sat in the shadow of Sandringham House, the 22,000-acre country retreat of the Queen herself.

It was in the churchyard of Sandringham that Diana's brother John had been buried. Often, as she grew up, Diana would visit her infant brother's grave, alone or with others. At times, it was a reminder to her that she was the girl who was supposed to have been a boy.

Diana's was a privileged upbringing, but not always a happy one. From birth she was provided with a nanny. While her two older sisters attended private classes in the family home, the infant Diana was cared for by her first and most beloved nanny, Judith Parnell.

These years were somewhat lonely for the young Diana. Her sisters, Sarah and Jane, had little time for her, and Diana didn't see as much of her mother or father as she would have liked.

Luckily for Diana, and for the family's future, a younger brother, Charles Spencer, was born when Diana was three years old. Brother Charles was christened in a lavish ceremony in Westminster Abbey, with the Queen herself as godmother.

Sarah and Jane were also honored to have the

Queen Mother as their godmother. Diana was the odd one out. She had been christened in the local church with two affluent commoners as godparents.

A plump and shy little girl, Diana continually felt herself a nuisance. She tried to make up for these feelings of failure by helping others. This sentiment would come back to her later in her life when her personal trials would lead her to become one of the world's bravest and most beloved humanitarians.

During much of Diana's childhood, it was her younger brother, Charles, who benefited from her compulsion to give. She often saw to both his physical and emotional needs.

Many mornings, Diana was the one who dressed Charles, and she tidied up his bedroom as well. Like all siblings, they had fights, but when young Charles was hurt or upset, it was Diana to whom he ran.

There were many material comforts for the Spencer children, but not nearly enough love or parental support, especially for the two youngest siblings.

"It was...a distant way of living from your parents," Diana's brother Charles would say later.

One of the most vivid recollections of Diana's life occurred in September 1967, when she was only six years old. That month her sisters, Sarah, age ten, and Jane, age fourteen, were sent away to boarding school at West Heath in Kent. Diana was suddenly without the older sisters she adored and tried her best to emulate.

But even more traumatic was the fact that, after a long and difficult marriage, her father and mother had decided on a trial separation. Diana would later vividly recall the day she watched her mother pack her bags and leave home forever.

The end of the Spencers' fourteen-year marriage was felt most strongly by Diana. Her two big sisters were already embarking on the next stage of their lives. And her little brother was too young to understand what was going on. Six-year-old Diana felt somehow responsible for her parents' divorce.

In the period leading up to the separation, Diana had witnessed several arguments between her father and mother. Some of those arguments were about the family's difficulty in producing a male heir, and Diana, overhearing these discussions, felt guilty for being "just a girl."

Soon after the separation, Diana's parents began fighting for control of their children. Diana's father insisted that they live with him at Park House, while her mother wanted them to live with her in London.

The end of the Spencer marriage had a lasting effect on Diana and her siblings.

"I remember my mother crying. Daddy never spoke to us about it," Diana would say later. "The whole thing was very unstable."

While there was little doubt that her parents loved their children, Diana would come to wonder if they ever really loved each other.

Diana decided at a very young age that she must love the man she married, and that he must love her in return.

Home, Sweet Home

After their parents' separation, Diana, Charles, and Sarah and Jane (when they were not at boarding school) remained with their father at Park House, though they often visited their mother in London.

As a little girl, Diana was quiet, reserved, and self-conscious. She was always polite and helpful to her parents, her siblings, and other children her own age, but she was restrained and aloof in front of strangers.

Often, in social situations, she would not speak at all unless spoken to. She and Charles had trouble making eye contact with others during conversation.

Diana, especially, had difficulty in meeting a stranger's gaze. She would speak in a quiet, steady voice, her eyes downcast.

With her family and friends, however, Diana acted very differently. With them, she displayed her strong, stubborn, mischievous streak—a rebellious spirit that would get her into trouble on occasion. Diana also had a wicked sense of humor.

This devilish, spirited side of Diana's personality remained hidden from all but the closest members of her immediate family and the nannies and servants who came to know her.

Diana adored her rambling childhood home. Park House possessed much character, and Diana knew every nook and cranny—from the flagstone kitchen, where the cook and Diana's cat, Marmaduke, struggled for domination, to her father's "Beatle Room," which was filled with psychedelic posters and other memorabilia of 1960s pop stars.

Only the gun room, filled with hunting rifles and trophies, remained locked and barred to the children, for reasons of safety.

But every other part of Park House was Diana's domain. As the most domestic of the Spencer girls, she often helped clean and care for the house she loved so dearly. Even years after she moved away, Diana would still return to visit her cherished childhood home.

Diana's bedroom at Park House was the nursery on the second floor. Rabbits, foxes, and even deer and elk lived in the surrounding woodlands. And because the coast of Norfolk was only a few miles away, seabirds often gathered outside Diana's bedroom window.

When she was ready to begin her formal education, Diana started to learn basic reading and writing, and a bit of history. Like her sisters, she did not attend school for the first few years. Instead, she, her brother Charles, and several other local children all took lessons from the Spencer governess, Miss Gertrude Allen—"Ally," as the children called her—in a schoolroom on the first floor of Park House.

Later, Diana would remember those first school days fondly. She would even invite her old governess to her royal wedding. Sadly, though, Diana would learn that Ally had passed away the year before.

For young Diana and Charles, starting their school day was great fun. No walking or school buses for them. Instead, they just slid down the banister of the impressive main stairway of Park House, right to the first floor, where Ally and their classmates were waiting!

Diana enjoyed the outdoors, especially in spring and summer, when Sarah and Jane returned from boarding school. Together the children would feed trout in the lake at Sandringham, play hide-and-seek in the huge garden, and take their dogs out for long walks in the forest nearby.

At the height of the summer season, the Spencer children liked to swim in their heated outdoor pool, which their father had built for them.

Diana especially excelled at swimming. She even had her own dive, which she called "the Spencer Special." The dive consisted of Diana climbing on

11

top of the pool's slide—which her father had forbidden her to do—then diving into the water so smoothly that she barely created a ripple.

The children also enjoyed attending the annual July fair, which was sponsored by their maternal grandmother, Ruth, Lady Fermoy. There were rides and attractions, contests, a flower show, and even live music.

At one fair, when Diana was nine, she won a goldfish in a ball toss contest. She brought the fish home and proudly placed it in a huge glass pitcher. The unfortunate fish had a short life, however. Diana's cat, Marmaduke, snatched it from the water and made a meal of it the very next day, when no one was looking!

Sometimes, on summer days, the younger children would hunt for newts and frogs. The Spencer girls would also ride horses, though Diana did not relish that pastime. Even years later, when she was grown, Diana would seldom get on a horse.

Her aversion to horseback riding could be traced to an incident when Diana was nine. Sarah and Jane had decided to go riding with their new governess, Mary Clarke. Diana, not to be outdone by the older sisters she adored, decided to join them. All went well at first. But as they approached the stables at the end of the ride, Diana's horse bolted and she fell off.

Her sisters teased her, and Diana, perhaps to

impress her sisters with her stiff upper lip, said she was not injured. Mary Clarke took her to a local doctor anyway, and he pronounced her fit.

A day later, Diana accompanied her mother on a ski trip to Switzerland. There, her arm felt numb and weak. A doctor was called in, and it was discovered that she had actually suffered a fracture in the fall from the horse. Her arm was placed in a splint.

A few weeks later, Diana's mother used the incident as evidence against her father in their ongoing custody battle.

Diana much preferred the beach to horses. She liked to picnic with her brother and sisters at their tiny private beach hut on the coast at Brancaster. The only catch was they had to remember to bring shovels along. Drifting sands would often bury the wooden beach hut, and the Spencer crew would have to dig the sand away before they could change clothes and have fun.

Diana particularly enjoyed spending time at the ocean, and especially that area of the British coast, which had a strange and wild beauty.

The tide would go out, leaving miles of empty sand where the ocean used to be—and the rusty hulk of a shipwreck visible in the distance. Then, with surprising swiftness, the tide would come back in, flooding the sandy plain and submerging the shipwreck once again.

The Spencer children thought the shipwreck

looked inviting to explore, but they were warned not to try to walk to it. It was farther away than it appeared, and if the tide came back, they would surely be drowned. So they had to settle for simply gazing at it from afar. The children spent most of these outings in the company of a governess or nanny.

Most of their meals at home, in fact, were taken upstairs, with the nanny. Once in a while, the children did dine with their father, in the downstairs dining room. But these tended to be stuffy, boring, formal affairs with little in the way of warmth.

This situation would change with the coming of another governess named Mary Clarke, but that was still in the future.

Despite this seeming lack of parental affection, Diana and her siblings were raised to be polite, honest, and accepting of others—no matter what their lot in life. The Spencer children were hardly aware that they were nobility, and accepted others for what they were, not for their titles.

"We never understood the whole title business," Charles once said. "I didn't even know I had any kind of title until I went to prep school. As children, we accepted our circumstances as normal."

With the natural beauty of the countryside where she was growing up, and the many woodland creatures that inhabited Norfolk, Diana became quite fond of animals.

From her earliest childhood, Diana would fill

her bed with a menagerie of stuffed animals, which she would fuss over and rearrange constantly. She even painted the eyes on one of her favorite stuffed toys with glow-in-the-dark paint. She felt it was watching and protecting her at night.

As she grew older, Diana acquired a succession of small pets, beginning with her cat, Marmaduke, which Charles and Jane both hated.

Soon, Diana would come to care for a succession of hamsters, rabbits, goldfish, and guinea pigs.

Her love of animals extended to an adult distaste of hunting for sport. Diana couldn't understand why anyone would want to hurt or kill an animal. Her feelings on this subject would, in time, put her at odds with members of the British nobility who enjoyed the royal tradition of the hunt—including her future husband, Prince Charles.

During this period of her childhood, Diana's mother fought for legal custody of her children. In Britain, as in the United States, the mother most often won this struggle. But because Diana's father was a titled nobleman, and because of a scandal surrounding her mother's divorce and subsequent romance with another man, the Spencer children—with the exception of Jane—spent most of their lives with their father.

Through all this difficulty, Johnnie Spencer tried to keep the divorce and custody battles hidden from his children. Nevertheless, the children were raised by a succession of nannies who changed often—

leaving Diana and Charles with unsettled feelings.

For some reason, Diana and Charles were both terribly afraid of the dark. When Diana was seven and her brother was four, both of them insisted on keeping a night-light glowing in the hallway and a candle flickering in their rooms at night.

In an interview many years later, Diana recalled listening to Charles crying for his mother one dark night, her own fear of the dark preventing her from leaving bed to comfort him.

"I could never pluck up enough courage to get out of bed," Diana would confess later.

But despite these nighttime fears, Diana's days were spent doing normal childhood activities, and she appeared to everyone who met her to be happy, busy, and filled with life. But had Diana really learned to cope with the upsetting breakdown of her parents' marriage? Or had she simply learned how to hide her feelings?

~~

Chapter 3

As Diana and Charles grew older, the seemingly endless parade of nannies and governesses put a difficult strain on the Spencer children.

Most of the domestic help hired by her father and mother were kind and considerate, but a number were not.

Shortly after her parents were divorced, Diana's mother caught one nanny placing laxatives in Sarah's food as punishment for her rebellious behavior. That nanny was promptly fired.

Another nanny struck Diana with a wooden spoon and banged her and her brother's heads together. She, too, was shown the door.

Although most of the nannies were kind and loving, and were remembered fondly by the Spencer children long after they left Park House, the constantly changing faces confused and frustrated the children.

Diana and her younger brother began to rebel against the succession of domestic help that were hired and then fired, or who moved on to other positions with other families.

Charles recalls an incident in which he was sent to his room as punishment for something he didn't do. His revenge was to kick a hole in his bedroom door.

But it was the high-spirited Diana who would prove to be the main problem for many of the domestic helpers hired by Johnnie Spencer to care for his children.

At times, Diana was urged to misbehave by her older sister Sarah, whom Diana tried to impress whenever possible. Diana hero-worshiped Sarah, and despite the gap in their ages, putting Diana together with Sarah often resulted in mischief.

On the other hand, Diana needed no encouragement to bedevil a nanny who stopped her from doing what she wanted to do. Once when a nanny refused to let Diana play outside because of bad weather, Diana decided to get even.

Playing outside was important to Diana. Charles didn't mind sitting in his room all day reading or staging battles with toy soldiers, but the indoors were *not* for Diana. She loved nothing more than to roam the woods around Park House with her dogs in tow.

So, to get her revenge on the nanny who kept her inside, Diana sneaked into the woman's room and threw her underclothes out the window, onto the roof of Park House!

As a final insult, Diana and her brother Charles went outside in the rain to watch the groundskeeper retrieve the nanny's underclothes. A short time later, the woman left the Spencers' employ in embarrassment.

On another occasion, Diana locked her nanny in the bathroom in an effort to stay awake past her bedtime. The poor woman was trapped, and wasn't set free until Diana's father came to say good night to his children and heard the unfortunate woman pounding on the bathroom door.

One of Sarah's and Diana's most fondly remembered animal pranks involved coaxing Charles's Shetland pony upstairs into the nursery for grooming. When the animal was discovered by the housemaid, Diana explained that she thought the pony was cold in the stables.

Everyone in the household wondered how the sisters had gotten the beast up the narrow, winding staircase. Diana explained that she lured the pony up the steps by dangling a carrot in front of its face!

Indeed, Diana was capable of great mischief. By the time she was nine years old, most of the nannies departed Park House precisely because of the pranks and behavior of Diana herself (although often urged on by Sarah).

In a way, such naughtiness was understandable for these children. To them, each new nanny was being hired to replace their missing mother, something they found hard to endure.

19

Diana reacted especially negatively if the nanny in question was young and pretty. If she was, Diana was immediately suspicious of her.

Soon, however, Diana and Charles were too old for the limited education they were receiving at home. They began classes at Silfield junior school, a small school about seven miles from Park House.

Classes at Silfield had a warm, family feel. Diana was still shy and self-conscious, but at least her friend Alexandra Lloyd attended the same classes. With Alexandra there, she didn't feel so lonely.

The Silfield school provided more than just an education. It offered social and fun activities for its pupils, including special "sports days" with fun competitions like three-legged races and weekly scavenger hunts.

The school's headmistress, Jean Lowe, did her best to provide a friendly atmosphere for her students. But Diana and her brother once again felt out of place. For one thing, they were the only children at the school whose parents were divorced. This situation led to some awkwardness on parent-teacher days, because Diana's father and mother refused to attend the same events.

Diana tried her best to fit in at Silfield. She was kind and considerate to the other children, especially those who were younger than she was.

Unfortunately, Diana was not a good student. Most of the time she seemed confused or bored by her lessons. Her governess at that time, Mary

Clarke, thought that Diana would rather be outside doing something than sitting around indoors. She was a very lively girl—perhaps too lively to be contained in a structured environment.

The one area in which Diana *did* excel was art. Diana loved to paint, and art was her favorite subject. During art class, Diana would paint with concentration, taking pride in her achievements. That was why her friends and teachers were so completely taken by surprise one day when Diana burst into tears in the middle of art class.

To those around her, there seemed no reason for such an outburst. Looking back on the incident now, it seems obvious that this was a very emotional time for the little girl.

Charles, meanwhile, was doing very well at Silfield. While Diana struggled to learn the basics, her brother breezed through his studies, remembering historical facts, math tables, and language lessons with ease.

This led to some fights between brother and sister. Because she was older and bigger, Diana usually won. But Charles would soon learn that he could outsmart his older sister. While Diana might trounce him physically, he could hurt her with words.

Charles began to tease his sister by calling her "Brian," the name of a dull-witted snail character on a popular British children's television show. Diana hated being called Brian and often cried over it.

Finally, the teasing got so bad that both Diana's

father and mother demanded that Charles stop using that name in his sister's presence.

While her schoolwork did not improve significantly while she attended Silfield, Diana did learn the basics, and the school provided some much-needed order and discipline in her chaotic life.

With time and familiarity, Diana learned to mix well with the other children. Soon she was seen by her teachers and friends as a cheerful, fun-loving child who was not affected by the trauma of her unstable home life and her parents' divorce.

But was Diana *really* not affected?

Chapter 4

New Beginnings

The pain and suffering that her parents' divorce caused Diana was not gone but was lodged deep inside her. Outwardly, she was a pleasant, tidy, well-behaved child who was considerate of others.

But inside she was confused and torn between two parents whom she genuinely loved and respected.

Sadly, there were daily situations that would remind Diana and Charles of how their lives had been changed forever by their parents' domestic strife.

The Spencer siblings could sense the growing rivalry between their mother and father for the children's affections. But when the children themselves craved love and attention, they were often disappointed. Both parents provided for the material needs of their children in a generous and lavish fashion, but hugs, kisses, and words of encouragement were much more rare—although far more desirable.

On Diana's seventh birthday, her father threw her an extravagant party, which included camel rides for the invited guests. At Christmas, they were presented with a catalog from Hamley's, a pricey toy store in London, and told to mark the gifts they wanted. Father Christmas *always* delivered exactly what the children wanted.

Diana's mother bought most of Diana's clothes. Often she would present her youngest daughter with fashionable dresses and blouses, but Diana did not favor such clothing. Instead, she copied her sister Sarah's look—which was heavy on blue jeans and flannel shirts.

Diana's fashion trendsetting days were still far off in the future.

But even her parents' generosity forced Diana to confront her parents' rivalry. In 1969, eight-year-old Diana was invited to the wedding of one of her cousins. For the occasion, her mother bought her a new green dress, while her father purchased for her an equally fashionable blue dress.

"I can't remember to this day which one I wore, but I remember being totally traumatized by it because it would show favoritism," Diana said of the incident.

Another constant reminder of their parents' estrangement were the frequent train trips Sarah, Jane, Diana, and Charles made between their father's home in Norfolk and their mother's home in London, Cadogan Place.

These trips often started out as exciting journeys filled with new sights, sounds, and surroundings. But the excursions, no matter how thrilling they began, almost always ended in tears and sadness.

"I don't want you to go tomorrow," Frances would sob as the time neared for Diana and Charles to return to Park House. Her emotional outbursts confused and upset her youngest children.

This scene would be repeated on holidays, which made otherwise festive seasons quite unsettling for Diana and Charles.

Things improved in 1969, when Frances introduced her children to her new husband, Peter Shand-Kydd, when the children arrived for a holiday stay with their mother.

Peter was immediately accepted by the children, and their mother's happiness was obvious to them all. Although this marriage did not end the legal wrangling over child custody, it did much to end the bitter rivalry between Diana's parents.

Diana was about to begin a new phase in her life. She was enrolled to attend Riddlesworth Hall, a boarding school two hours' drive from Park House.

If her parents had any fears that she would not thrive away from home, they proved to be groundless. By the end of her first year at boarding school (which she began at the same time as her friend Alexandra Lloyd), Diana was happy and content. She made many new friends and was proud of her accomplishments.

Riddlesworth was an unusual boarding school. Pupils were treated like members of the family, and students were even permitted to bring a pet. Diana, of course, brought her beloved guinea pig, Peanuts. Unfortunately, girls were only allowed to bring along one stuffed animal, so she had to be content with her favorite green hippo.

In her first year at Riddlesworth, she won the prized Legatt Cup, which was awarded to the student who was the most helpful around the school. She also developed a lifelong love of dance.

At Riddlesworth, Diana became a popular pupil. Loud and fun-loving in the dorm, Diana remained quiet and reserved in class. Though she didn't like to be the center of attention, she forced herself to do things that would help her overcome her shyness.

In time, Diana even agreed to appear in the school play. True to her reserved nature, however, she insisted on playing a Dutch doll—a part which did not require speaking.

As Diana entered her teenage years, she showed a new maturity. At home, she washed and ironed her own clothes and tidied up not only her little brother's room but her oldest sister Sarah's room as well. This was quite a chore, as Sarah was very messy.

Diana also played dress-up with her oldest sister's clothes. Despite her new maturity, she still worshiped and emulated her oldest sister.

Diana seemed destined to follow in her sisters' footsteps. Soon she was enrolled at West Heath boarding school in Kent, which both of her older sisters had attended before her.

But which sister would Diana emulate? Her competitive, tempestuous oldest sister, Sarah, or the more serious, contemplative Jane?

To no one's surprise, she began West Heath acting much like Sarah. She disrupted classes and was nearly expelled when she sneaked away from the dorm one night to buy candy for the other girls.

The incident was considered so serious that her parents were called to West Heath. But to Diana's surprise, her mother openly expressed admiration for her daughter's newfound spirit.

"I didn't know you had it in you," Frances told Diana after the incident.

Diana became quite popular at West Heath. She was often challenged to eating contests by the other students, and she accepted their dares with a laugh.

Soon she was known as a "bubbly character" who was "full of life." The secret, mischievous side of Diana, which she usually revealed only to her family, was now moving to the forefront.

Diana had flowered into a feisty, if somewhat gawky, teenager who often bowed her head down to hide her height. She enjoyed her time at West Heath immensely. The only disappointment in her life was her average academic performance. Both of

27

her sisters had excelled in that area, and their brother Charles was demonstrating the academic skills that would later take him to the renowned Oxford University.

But things were not altogether bleak for Diana at school. She loved history and excelled in essay writing and the study of literature—though for entertainment, Diana preferred the romance novels of Barbara Cartland over more serious works.

Another area where Diana excelled was in helping others. West Heath encouraged its students to do good works, and it was there that Diana began the charity work for which she would, in time, become world-famous.

It seemed as if life for young Diana Spencer was finally becoming calm and stable. But soon more upheavals and changes would threaten her newfound peace of mind. And one threat would come from an unexpected source—a new rival for her father's affections.

Chapter 5

The "Wicked" Stepmother

Of the three Spencer girls, Diana seemed closest to
her father as she was growing up.

Sarah was her own woman—a fiery redhead
who was totally independent. Jane spent most of her
free time with her mother at Cadogan Place in
London. Charles, like all little boys, loved his
mother and tried to be like his father, whom he
loved and admired. But Diana was the apple of her
father's eye.

Although Johnnie Spencer had expressed some
disappointment at first when Diana was born, the
birth of Charles had provided him finally with a
male heir. The emotional barrier between father and
daughter was now gone. In fact, as Diana grew
older, he seemed to favor her.

But all of the Spencer sisters rallied together
when they felt threatened by a stranger whom they
perceived to be stealing their father's affections.
That incident occurred in the summer of 1972, when
Diana was eleven. But the consequences of that

29

moment would affect all of the Spencers for many years to come.

It was Sarah, the oldest, who first noted the amount of time their father was spending with a woman named Raine, Lady Dartmouth, who had four children of her own and who lived in London.

Lord Althorp (Johnnie Spencer) had met Lady Dartmouth at a charity ball, and the two became fast friends.

But Sarah sensed there was something deeper going on between her father and this stranger than mere friendship. So when Lord Althorp invited Lady Dartmouth to lunch, so she could meet his three daughters and son, Sarah decided it was a good opportunity to take up a position against this interloper.

The meal began innocently enough, though Sarah had already planted the seeds of suspicion in the minds of Jane and Diana. Charles, still young and uncomplicated, remained aloof from the struggle.

Raine, Lady Dartmouth, was the daughter of romance writer Barbara Cartland, Diana's favorite author. But this connection did not protect the woman from the jealousy of the Spencer girls, including Diana.

Like her famous mother, Lady Dartmouth was something of a character. One of her colleagues in London said of her, "She's not a person, she's an experience." While Barbara Cartland preferred to dress entirely in pink, Raine's look was more traditional—but no less formal.

On the day of the lunch, Lady Dartmouth arrived at Park House with a rigid hairstyle and impeccable dress. She was calm and reserved, but she struck young Diana, especially, as comical.

Though Diana stifled her laughter, and maintained a polite demeanor throughout the lunch, Sarah had other ideas. At first she tried to make a few impolite comments in the hope of angering Lady Dartmouth. But the woman was too canny to fall into Sarah's trap. When verbal barbs failed to shake Raine, Sarah resorted to out-and-out rudeness.

As lunch was drawing to a close, Sarah took a deep breath and, to everyone's great shock, belched loudly.

"Sarah!" Lord Althorp cried, appalled at his daughter's lack of manners.

Sarah just smiled and explained that burping was considered a sign of appreciation in Arab countries. But her father was not fooled, and he promptly banished her from the table. Diana jumped to the defense of her sister, and was chastised by her father. She soon excused herself, claiming illness.

Since their father seldom scolded his children, and almost never in front of a relative stranger, the Spencer girls had to know that Raine held a special place in their father's heart.

It was obvious to everyone at Park House that if Lord Althorpe had set his hat on finding a new wife, the unfortunate woman would have to put up with a lot from his protective daughters!

In time, Diana and her sisters became less concerned with their father's friendship with Lady Dartmouth. There were other tragic and unsettling developments in their lives—including the death of Diana's beloved maternal grandmother in 1972, and the death of the Earl of Althorp, her paternal grandfather, in 1975.

Though Diana was quite fond of her grandmother, the death of her grandfather ultimately affected her more. With her grandfather's passing, her father, Johnnie Spencer, the Lord Althorp, inherited the title of earl. With it came a huge family estate outside of London called Althorp Hall.

In the summer of 1975, the Spencer family moved to Althorp Hall, leaving the country life at Park House behind forever.

It was a sad time for fourteen-year-old Diana. She loved Park House, and when she returned from boarding school that summer, the first sight that greeted her were packing crates all over the front yard.

With the move, and Johnnie Spencer's ascent to the earldom, came new troubles for the Spencers. The family was suddenly strapped for money, and the new responsibilities of his title required Diana's father to find other ways to support his family.

In this, he was helped by Raine, Lady
Dartmouth. Johnnie Spencer, the new Earl, married
her in 1977 without telling his children of his
plans—just as Diana's mother had done when she
remarried. But where the children immediately
accepted their new stepfather, they would never
come to terms with the woman they nicknamed
"Acid Raine."

Raine had a considerable personal fortune and
superb business and organizational skills. Within a
few years, she had reorganized some of the Earl's
assets and sold off some of the art in Althorp Hall,
so that by 1978 the family was financially secure for
the first time.

But the children's animosity toward Raine did
not stop. Sarah and Jane, especially, remained hostile toward their new stepmother. Diana, who was
more adaptable than her sisters, accepted Raine,
even if she didn't particularly like the new woman
in her father's life. This time out, however, brother
Charles was not so aloof. He joined the chorus of his
eldest sisters, stating that he "didn't like her one
bit."

In time, Diana graduated from West Heath. And
again, she followed sister Sarah's footsteps by
enrolling at the Institut Alpin Videmanette, an
expensive finishing school in Switzerland. Students
there were expected to learn poise and speak nothing but French all day.

At the Institut, Diana studied domestic science,

dressmaking, and cookery. Enrolled at the same time was Diana's friend Sophie Kimball. The friends ignored the rules and spoke English to each other, and spent more time skiing than on their studies.

Diana felt stifled and oppressed by finishing school. She wrote home constantly, pleading with her father to allow her to leave. Finally, he relented, and Diana ended her formal education.

In her time away from home, Diana had blossomed. She was still shy and somewhat overweight. But when Diana made plans to live and work in London—where her sister Sarah was living—their mutual acquaintances saw the future princess much differently than before.

"Suddenly the insignificant ugly duckling was obviously going to be a swan," her brother Charles said of Diana.

❤❤ ────────────────────────────

Chapter 6

Free at Last

Diana was desperate to begin living on her own. Though she was still only a teenager, she was determined to start her new, independent life.

Unfortunately, Diana had few marketable skills and no formal education beyond finishing school. Unless she was very lucky, she was doomed to an uncertain future working at menial, unskilled jobs. Despite her title and her family's wealth, Diana needed a job to survive.

But what to do?

Diana certainly knew what she was *expected* to do. Like most young women of her background, she was supposed to find a well-to-do husband. And it would be even better if he was an aristocrat.

But Diana, the ugly duckling who had turned into a swan, had other ideas. The young woman who long ago told governess Mary Clarke that her only goal in life was to find a husband and have babies now wanted to stretch her wings.

Diana might have obtained a modeling job if she had had the confidence and determination to pursue one. She certainly possessed beauty, as well as poise and manners gleaned from her aristocratic upbringing. But at sixteen, Diana (who would eventually become one of the most photographed women in the world) considered herself too tall and plump for so glamorous a career!

Luckily, Diana was offered a job in Hampshire with friends of her family. She was hired to cook, clean house, and look after the family's infant daughter. The job came with a room in the family home, so Diana accepted.

Three months later, her mother offered her a room at her home in Cadogan Square, London. Diana, now almost seventeen, jumped at the offer. Since her mother spent most of her time in Scotland, Diana had the place to herself.

It was like a dream come true. Diana practically had her own place in the heart of London! It was a heady amount of freedom for a teenage girl.

But to no one's surprise, Diana used her new-found independence wisely.

She immediately signed up with several temporary employment services. She worked as a waitress at private, catered parties. The future Princess of Wales also took on jobs cleaning houses and washing clothes. She was also hired as a babysitter for married friends and acquaintances.

During this period, Diana had a lively social life. While she didn't go to fashionable nightclubs or discos, or even drink for that matter, Diana was a frequent guest at dinner parties held by her married and single friends. She met a number of eligible bachelors at these affairs, but none overly impressed her.

On weekends, Diana traveled to Althorp to visit her father. If her father was busy, Diana would visit her sister Jane, in her private residence on the Althorp estate. Diana also traveled with her circle of friends and was fond of visiting their homes.

In September 1978, Diana visited the Norfolk home of a friend. When one of her hosts inquired about her father's health, Diana replied that she somehow sensed he was going to "drop down" in some way.

"If he dies, he will die immediately," she announced. "Otherwise, he will survive."

The next morning Diana learned that her father had suffered a massive stroke and was near death. Suddenly, she had to face the possibility of life without her beloved father.

Diana rushed to her father's side, where she was joined by her brother Charles, who came from Eton, her sisters, Jane and Sarah, and their stepmother, Raine. Doctors warned the family that the Earl was not expected to survive the night.

The children camped out in the hospital waiting room for the vigil. Three days later, a specialist announced that there was some hope. Diana's father was moved to a hospital better suited to care for him. There, he lay in a coma for three months.

To the children's surprise, it was Raine who

saved him. She searched for a cure for his illness, and learned of a new drug available in Germany. The drug was administered, and the Earl of Althorp awakened. In the following months, he slowly began to recover.

It was a harrowing time for the future Princess. During her father's long illness, her oldest sister, Sarah, often argued with Raine. Charles, too, felt that his stepmother was overbearing. But none of them could deny that her cure had worked or that the Earl was alive because his wife had stayed by his side.

During her father's long illness, Diana went back and forth to the hospital, even though she was often barred from visiting him, since he was unconscious most of the time. Her intense worries led her into bouts of binge eating. This, coupled with a cooking course she'd enrolled in, caused Diana to gain weight.

As her father began to recover, Diana was offered another job. This time it was giving young girls ballet lessons. The job combined Diana's two great loves, dancing and children, so she happily took it.

Diana was well suited to this work, and her supervisor, the legendary dance teacher Betty Vacani, was happy with Diana's talents and abilities. But a serious accident on a skiing vacation ended Diana's career as a dance instructor. It took her over three months to recover from injuries she suffered to tendons in her foot.

Soon Diana turned eighteen. Her father had promised Diana that she could have her own place in London when she came of age. The Earl was as good as his word. In July 1979, he presented Diana with her very own $85,000 apartment.

Diana, in turn, had promised her friends that they would always have a room with her. As she set about decorating her new home, many friends from her past roomed with her for various periods of time.

Diana enjoyed her role as landlady to her friends. She had the words *Chief Chick* painted on her bedroom door, and organized the housework so that no one was stuck doing all the chores. Later, as Princess, Diana would remember this period as the liveliest and most enjoyable time in her life.

Diana soon found a new job to go with her new home—one that suited her perfectly.

For three days a week, she worked at the Young England Kindergarten at St. Saviour's church hall. There, Diana taught dance, drawing, and painting. She joined the children in sing-alongs and games.

On Tuesdays and Thursdays, Diana looked after the young son of an American oil executive living in London. And she continued to clean her older sister's home in Chelsea.

Evenings were spent with her friend Carolyn Bartholomew. Sometimes Diana and Carolyn would indulge themselves in childish pranks. The girls would dash off in the middle of the night to ring doorbells, put tape over car and door locks, or, in one instance, "flour and egg" the car of a young man Diana thought had snubbed her. They also sometimes staged raids on their friends' apartments.

It was during this lively period that Diana began to date. She went out with aristocratic young men, most of them graduates of Eton, where her brother was attending school.

"Diana is an uptown girl who has never gone for downtown men," said Rory Scott, a friend from that period.

Though she was popular, Diana did not see any one young man in particular. She mostly joined her friends and a group of boys for supper at bistros, a night at the theater, or on day trips.

And then in the fall of 1979, Diana received an unexpected invitation from the royal family. She was asked to attend a shooting weekend in February at Sandringham, the Queen's country retreat near Diana's childhood home.

Diana announced her good fortune to her friend, Lucinda Harvey, while she was on her knees washing the floor.

"Gosh," Lucinda replied. "Perhaps you are going be the next Queen of England."

Diana laughed and continued to scrub the floor. "Can you see me swanning around in kid gloves and a ball gown?"

Chapter 7

A Royal Romance

Although neither of them remembered the occasion, Diana first met her future husband when she was just a baby. It happened during the winter of 1961, when twelve-year-old Charles, Prince of Wales, was visiting his mother's Sandringham retreat.

At the time, young Prince Charles barely glanced at the tiny baby sleeping in her cot. After all, what twelve-year-old boy is interested in babies?

But the Prince would eventually take a very keen interest in *this* particular baby—it would just take some time.

In fact, it would be sixteen years before Prince Charles and Lady Diana Spencer would meet again. The encounter took place in the middle of a farmer's field during a shooting party in November 1977.

It was a cold, rainy, bleak afternoon when sixteen-year-old Diana, dressed in a borrowed parka that was too large for her, boots, and blue jeans, crossed the field to meet the heir to the British throne.

It was almost twilight when the two came face to face near Nobottle Woods.

"What a sad man," Diana thought when she first saw him. The future Princess was intrigued to finally meet the most eligible bachelor in England, though she was not impressed with his five-foot-ten-inch height, thinking to herself that she would tower over him in high heels. But Diana would later say that she admired his beautiful blue eyes.

The Prince later remarked that he thought Diana was "a very jolly and attractive" girl, "full of fun," though Diana herself believed that "he barely noticed me at all."

At that time, Prince Charles was dating Diana's sister Sarah. Their relationship lasted for about nine months. During that time, there was speculation in the British press that Lady Sarah Spencer might become the Princess of Wales.

But something happened that ended Sarah's relationship with the Prince.

In February 1978, Charles invited Sarah on a ski trip. After the vacation, Sarah spoke to the press about her relationship with Prince Charles. She told a magazine interviewer that she thought of the Prince as "the big brother I never had."

The words were innocent enough, but Sarah had broken an unwritten code: Never talk about the royal family to the press.

Sarah's relationship with the Prince faded after that, but she was still close enough to Charles to be invited to his thirtieth birthday party at Buckingham Palace in November 1978.

To Sarah's surprise, her sister Diana was invited, too.

Diana, it was discovered later, first came to the attention of the royal family when she acted as a bridesmaid for her sister Jane's wedding that April. It was the first major social occasion that Diana attended as a young woman, and many of the royals were surprised at how beautiful and mature the once-gawky girl had become.

Even the Queen Mother, Prince Charles's grandmother, noticed Diana's beauty, grace, and charm. She complimented the Earl on the fine job he had done in bringing Diana up.

It is easy to believe that, behind the scenes, there was some royal matchmaking going on. Prince Charles was, after all, now thirty—an age he once said was a good time to marry. And the monarchy needed an heir to the throne.

In short, Prince Charles, as the future King of England, was expected to marry and have children. He'd been looking for some time now, but he had yet to find his princess—a woman who would not only fit the glass slipper of exacting royal standards, but be willing to wear it through the often difficult demands of royal life. So it came as no surprise to later discover that the beloved Queen Mother herself suggested to Charles that he invite Diana as well as her sisters to his birthday bash.

Regardless of what got her there, Diana managed to impress the Prince of Wales's family that glorious evening. Charles's escort that night was the actress Susan George, but the eyes of his royal parents and grandparents were on seventeen-year-old Lady Diana Spencer.

Even though she was described by another guest that night as having "mousy hair and puppy fat," Lady Diana had other qualities that made her a worthy candidate, in the Queen Mother's eyes, for the role of Princess and future Queen.

The timing was not yet right for the couple, but the Queen Mother and her longtime friend Ruth, Lady Fermoy, Diana's maternal grandmother, were already making plans.

In August 1979, tragedy struck the royal family. Lord Mountbatten, hero of the Second World War and confidant to Prince Charles, was murdered in Ireland when terrorists planted a bomb aboard his fishing boat. The royal family, especially Charles, was devastated. The Prince had lost his closest friend and adviser—the man he called his second father.

In the aftermath of the murder, Charles began to realize the enormousness of the role he was born to play. He began to sense more meaningfully the need to end his bachelor days. It was time to find a suitable bride. And indeed, his mother and grandmother were both urging him to marry.

The stage was set. Charles and Diana were about

to embark on a path that would eventually lead them to the steps of St. Paul's Cathedral.

It was a chance meeting in the stables belonging to a friend of Prince Philip, the husband of Queen Elizabeth and Prince Charles's father, where Diana and Prince Charles had their first meaningful conversation.

Charles had just finished playing polo and was resting his horse when he sat down next to Diana on a bale of hay. They spoke for the first time that day, and Diana expressed her condolences for the death of Lord Mountbatten.

Diana told Prince Charles that he had looked so sad at Mountbatten's funeral. She told him that when she watched his suffering from afar, "my heart bled for you."

Diana's gentle sincerity touched the Prince, and they spoke together far into the evening. By the time they parted that night, Diana was surprised by the attention the Prince, twelve years her senior, had paid to her.

Prince Charles was so impressed by Diana's compassionate words that he asked her to accompany him back to Buckingham Palace the next morning. She declined, because it would be rude to her host to leave so suddenly.

Still, even after this chance meeting, Diana did not have romantic feelings for Prince Charles. And she was sure that he did not think of her in that way, either.

45

A short time later, Prince Charles sent his valet to hand-deliver a formal invitation for Diana to accompany him that very evening to the opera and a late-night dinner at the palace.

Though she was flustered, and the invitation came at such short notice, Diana accepted. She and her roommate, Carolyn Bartholomew, hurried to dress and prepare Diana for her big date. The evening was a success, and an invitation to a party on the royal yacht came soon after.

Diana felt intimidated by the older, wiser, and more worldly Charles. But she had little time to contemplate her misgivings before an invitation to the Queen's Highland castle in Balmoral, Scotland, arrived.

Diana was worldly enough to understand that this invitation to the Windsor family seat was a test. If she managed to pass, her future with Charles was assured, as long as it was what they both wanted.

Although she was intimidated by the crowd at Balmoral, Diana was wise enough not to stay in the castle itself. She asked for, and was granted, an invitation to stay with her sister Jane and her young husband at their cottage on the Balmoral estate.

The Prince visited Diana there every day, offering to escort her to a barbecue, or extending an invitation for a long walk in the woods.

One day, Charles asked Diana to go fishing with him. They were having a fine time talking and shar-

The young
Lady Diana
Spencer.

Nineteen-year-old
kindergarten teacher Diana Spencer
poses with two of her students.

Prince Charles and Princess Diana
on their wedding day, July 29, 1981.

Diana and Charles meet with reporters a few weeks after their wedding.

An expectant Diana awaits the birth of her first child in 1982.

The proud parents leave the hospital after the birth of Prince William.

Princess Diana
and Prince Charles
during happier
times.

Diana dances at the White House with
John Travolta in 1985. The ink-blue velvet gown
she wore was sold for $222,500 at a charity
auction in New York City in 1997.

Diana running
in the annual
sports meet for
parents at the
Wetherby School
in 1989. She
came in second.

Diana, Charles,
and their sons pose for a family portrait.

This portrait
of the Princess,
by Patrick
Demarchelier,
was commissioned
by *Vogue* for its
December 1990
issue.

Diana stands out at Ascot.

She
captivated
us.

Visiting with an AIDS patient at Middlesex Hospital in 1991.

Diana shakes hands during a visit to Zimbabwe in July 1993.

March 1993. Princess Diana makes her first official visit to Nepal, following her formal separation from Prince Charles.

The Princess in the Play Centre
at the Great Ormand Street
Children's Hospital in London.

Princess Diana
greeting a child
with leprosy
at the Sitanala
Leprosy Hospital in
Indonesia.

Diana at a hospice in Calcutta.

Princess Diana holds hands with Mother Teresa after a meeting at the Missionaries of Charity's residence in the Bronx section of New York City.

Diana visits with children at the Shri Swaminarayan Mandir Hindu Mission in June 1997.

Princess Diana, flanked by Henry Kissinger (left) and General Colin Powell, receives the Humanitarian of the Year award from the Cerebral Palsy Foundation in New York City, on November 12, 1995.

Princess Diana arrives in Luanda, the capital of Angola, a country where 9 million land mines—almost one per person—still lie in wait for victims.

Princess Diana explores minefields during her visit to Angola in January 1997.

The Princess
spending time
with a patient
at the Neves
Bendinha
Orthopaedic
Centre in
Angola.

Diana visits
the Children's
Casualty
Centre at the
Northwick
Park Hospital
in London in
July 1997.

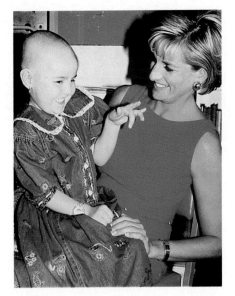

Prior to the tragedy that claimed their mother's life, Princes William and Harry pose for photographers while vacationing in Scotland in August 1997.

Mourners spontaneously created a sea of flowers
in Diana's memory at Kensington Palace.

All over the
world, people
mourned the
death of Diana.
In New York
City, a shrine
was created
outside the
British
Consulate.

Farewell, sweet princess.

ing their thoughts when Diana noticed a man hiding in the bushes, spying on them.

It was a news photographer. He was trying to get a picture of the Prince of Wales and his new romantic interest. Diana hid behind a tree and later vanished into the woods, foiling the photographer's attempts to get a picture.

This scene was but a foreshadowing of the glaring and often unrelenting public spotlight that Diana would soon step into. In time, photographers and journalists would follow her every move, snapping pictures of every public and private moment.

Back at work in her kindergarten class, Diana was surprised to find photographers waiting for her when she escorted the children outside for recess. She finally agreed to have her picture taken, on the condition that the photographers agree to leave her alone after that.

Unknown to Diana, the strong sunlight was behind her, making her long cotton skirt seem invisible. The next morning, pictures of her, with the silhouette of her long legs clearly visible, were splashed across newspapers all over Britain. She received some gentle teasing over the incident from the Prince.

"I knew your legs were good, but I didn't know they were *that* spectacular," he told her.

Soon Diana was being followed by journalists everywhere she went. Her phone rang late at night, as reporters called her for a statement or for some fresh gossip. Diana managed to keep the press at bay, never offering to comment on the Prince, as her sister Sarah had done to her regret.

In desperation, Diana contacted the press office at Buckingham Palace. They told her she was on her own as far as dealing with the press. She was not a member of the royal family, so she could not expect their help.

Though Diana enjoyed the company of Charles, she wasn't sure the feelings she had toward him were love. She had never had a real boyfriend, so she could not measure her feelings against experience.

Her grandmother, Ruth, Lady Fermoy, who at first seemed to push Diana into Charles's path, now cautioned her granddaughter on the perils of marrying into the royal family.

But it was too late. The more Diana saw Charles, the more she fell in love with him. Soon she could not even imagine her life without him. But still, Diana had doubts about the people surrounding Charles, especially a woman by the name of Camilla Parker-Bowles, whom he had once dated.

When Charles went to Switzerland for a ski vacation, Diana missed him terribly. He called her after a day or two, and told Diana that when he returned to England, he had something important to ask her.

He arrived home on February 3, 1981. Three

days later, he arranged to see Diana at Windsor Castle. Late that evening, while Prince Charles was showing Diana the nursery, he asked her to marry him.

To his surprise, Diana treated his proposal as a joke. She actually giggled. But soon she could see that Prince Charles was serious. Despite an insistent voice inside her head that told her she would never be Queen, she accepted his proposal.

Diana told Prince Charles over and over that she loved him.

"Whatever 'love' means," was his reply.

Chapter 8

The Wedding of the Century

The stage was set for the royal wedding of the century. Diana knew she had a tremendous amount of planning to do, so she and her mother set off for a sheep station in New South Wales, Australia, to hide out from the press and prepare for her wedding.

The British press searched far and wide for Diana, but her location was a secret to all but the Prince of Wales. As the days passed, however, Charles failed to call Diana. Finally, Diana called him, only to learn that he was out of town.

Charles called the next morning and apologized for not ringing sooner. But Diana had had her first inkling that she was not as important to her future husband as he was to her.

When she returned to London, a bouquet of flowers was delivered to her door. The gift was from Charles. There was no note attached to it. Again, Diana was plagued by doubts about her handsome Prince.

Her misgivings were dispelled when Charles

invited her to the home of Nick Gaselee, his personal horse trainer. She had an enjoyable time, until Charles mounted his favorite horse, Allibar.

It was then that Diana suddenly experienced another of her strange premonitions. She announced that the horse was going to have a heart attack and die. Allibar did just that, seconds later. Charles was saddened by the loss of his beloved mount, and the rest of the day was very bleak for them both.

The night before her engagement to Charles was to be officially announced, Diana packed her bags, hugged her roommates, and left her apartment forever. She would live alone in Buckingham Palace for the next three months until the wedding. Then Diana and Charles would move into the Prince's private quarters in Kensington Palace.

A Scotland Yard inspector arrived to escort her to the palace. In a quiet moment, he told Diana that this was the last night of freedom in her life.

"Make the most of it," the policeman urged her.

The words made the young Princess-in-waiting realize that her privacy was now a thing of the past. But in truth, Diana's private life had ended weeks before. She had been pursued by the press no matter where she went.

It was hard for Diana at the palace. She felt isolated from her friends and stifled by the somber atmosphere of the royal household.

"She went to live in Buckingham Palace, and

then the tears started," remarked Carolyn Bartholomew, Diana's former roommate.

The pressure of the coming nuptials weighed heavily on Diana. She began to lose weight. Her waist shrank from twenty-nine inches to twenty-three inches in a few weeks. During this stressful period, Diana's bulimia began in earnest. She would not overcome this dangerous eating disorder until a decade later.

Diana soon realized that her personal wardrobe was totally unsuited to life at the palace. She contacted a friend at *Vogue* magazine and asked her for fashion advice. Soon a host of famous fashion designers was knocking at Diana's door.

But Diana's choice of clothes did not always impress her Prince. At their first formal affair as a couple, Diana wore a black strapless dress that accented her stunning figure.

Charles did not like the dress and told Diana that black was only for people in mourning. She replied that she had no other suitable dress. Off they went to the ball, where a battery of photographers awaited them. The disagreement over her fashion sense had already undermined Diana's confidence.

At the dance, Diana was introduced to Princess Grace of Monaco, the former actress Grace Kelly. The glamorous Princess Grace noticed young Diana's discomfort and the reaction of others to her outfit.

The Princess led the Princess-to-be to the ladies'

room, where Diana expressed her uncertainty about royal life and her fears about the future.

"Don't worry," Princess Grace replied. "It will get a lot worse."

Sadly, Princess Grace was to die in a car crash eighteen months later. Princess Diana would attend her funeral, sitting next to First Lady Nancy Reagan, wife of the president of the United States, Ronald Reagan.

During those months before the wedding, Diana was charming and composed in public. Privately, however, she began to have doubts about her future as the Princess of Wales.

She was especially concerned about her husband-to-be's relationship with Camilla Parker-Bowles. Diana wondered if there was not some deeper relationship between the Prince and the older, married Camilla.

On July 29, 1981, the morning of her wedding, Diana rose and looked out her window at the huge crowds below. They were waiting to witness the wedding procession. As make-up artists and fashion designers David and Elizabeth Emanuel dressed and fussed over her, Diana began "the most emotionally confusing day" of her life.

Diana's father, still weak from his stroke, expressed his pride. But as they moved to the glass coach, in which father and daughter would ride to St. Paul's Cathedral, they realized with horror that the long train on Diana's ivory silk wedding gown would not fit into the horse-drawn carriage! The gown was stuffed into the coach, but it was badly crushed.

At the cathedral, as Diana moved down the aisle on her father's arm, she was filled with love for her Prince. But her persistent doubts refused to be banished, despite the Archbishop of Canterbury's words that her marriage was "the stuff of which fairy tales are made."

But as the final vows were spoken, and the Princess of Wales heard the cheers of her subjects, Diana managed to convince herself that her fairy tale had come true, and that she would live happily ever after.

Chapter 9

Happily Ever After?

There's a good reason why fairy tales end when the couple exchanges wedding vows and rides off into the sunset. A happy ending is always certain.

If Diana's story had ended on her wedding day, her story would have been a very happy one. Everyone who watched the lavish ceremony believed that the Prince and Princess's married life would be as joyful as their wedding—a wonderful dream come true.

Sadly, this was not to be.

Diana's married life seemed to begin happily enough. Shortly after the wedding ceremony, the newlyweds greeted a cheering crowd from a balcony at Buckingham Palace. There, in front of the world—and with the Queen's permission—a dashing Prince Charles kissed Diana on the lips.

"That's the picture that will seal the romance of the monarchy for twenty years," said a palace press aide.

Then the long honeymoon began. The Prince and Princess of Wales left London by train. They spent the first days of their marriage on the late Lord Mountbatten's estate. From there they went on a cruise of the Mediterranean aboard the royal yacht *Britannia*.

Diana had been looking forward to her honeymoon. She expected to finally have some time alone with her new Prince. After all, weren't honeymoons supposed to be the time when a new husband and wife could be alone together?

Unfortunately, Diana soon realized that this was not a normal honeymoon. She was seldom alone with her Prince on the royal yacht. Meals were black-tie affairs shared with two dozen ship's officers. Even when the royal couple stayed in their private compartments, a Royal Marine band played outside their door!

Diana mixed well with the crew of the *Britannia*. She even sang songs with the sailors. But her binge eating still haunted her. She would creep into the galley at odd hours to consume bowls of ice cream and other treats.

When the honeymoon was over, Diana returned to England expecting that the public would soon tire of her. That was not to be. The shy girl from Norfolk found herself on the cover of every magazine in the world. In time, she would become the most photographed person in history. Diana would grace the covers of forty-four issues of *People* magazine alone.

But right now, Diana had a new job to learn.

Unfortunately, she had to learn it *while* she was doing it, which made for some mistakes.

Some tricks she picked up from other royal women, like putting tiny weights in the hem of her skirts so that the wind would not blow them up.

From the British Special Air Services—the British equivalent of the U.S. Navy SEALs and the Special Forces combined—Diana learned how to handle herself in dangerous situations. These courses were called anti-terrorism training. One particularly realistic lesson included driving her own car through an elaborate course with flash grenades and smoke bombs exploding all around her.

The Princess was even taught how to use a .38mm pistol and a machine gun!

Diana found it easy to talk and joke with people like the servants in the royal households and the sailors on the royal yacht. Where the new Princess had trouble, though, was in getting along with other royalty.

Diana was the kind of Princess no one had ever seen before. Before she married her Prince, she had actually had jobs and lived in the real world. In many ways, she was the exact opposite of her husband.

Diana found it difficult to follow palace protocol—the royal rules of what to do and how to do it. Diana described herself as the kind of person who didn't go by a rule book, the kind who led with her heart and not her head. But royal protocol required that she remember many details about how to act and what to say.

For example, she learned that when people were introduced to her, they must first address her as "Your Royal Highness," and, from then on, as "Ma'am." The Princess, who had had a number of nicknames such as "Brian," "Duch," and "Squidgy," suddenly had to respond to "Your Highness."

It was a jolting transition for a girl who had been cleaning houses for a living just a year ago!

In front of the cameras, Diana was charming and composed. Outside the media glare, Diana continued to love Charles. They went on long walks together and discussed his favorite books. And when Charles was away on royal business, he wrote tender and emotional love letters to his new bride. Diana even had an affectionate nickname for her Prince.

She called him "Hubcap."

Early in the marriage, Charles tried to help his wife adjust to her new status. On an official visit to Wales, Charles guided his new bride through the bewildering maze of protocol. It was also on this trip that the couple learned which one of them was the more popular.

When meeting with the people, it is the custom for a royal couple to separate, each one taking the opposite side of the street to greet the crowds. When Diana chose one side of the street, the people on the opposite side collectively groaned in disappointment.

Charles smiled wryly and apologized to the people he was greeting by telling them that he was sorry he didn't have more wives to go around!

But in this crucial period, which Diana would later call the Dark Ages, she received little help or support from the rest of the royal family, with the exception of Princess Margaret, the Queen's sister.

"Margo," as Diana called her, always had a kind word or some helpful advice for her. But Princess Margaret also had her own royal duties, and she was seldom there to assist the new Princess.

Soon Diana's eating disorder, bulimia nervosa, became more pronounced. The stress of their wedding, the subsequent honeymoon in the glare of the public spotlight, and the return to new responsibilities, aggravated her condition. Diana continued to lose weight, until she looked frail and sickly.

Bulimia was what led Diana to binge-eat when there was stress in her life. She would then make herself sick and vomit up the food. At the height of her illness, Diana was eating and purging four or five times a day.

Because of her poise, charm, and beauty, the people on the royal staff easily forgot that Diana was not yet twenty-one. She was barely out of her teens, facing a host of duties that would be difficult for an adult to handle. But, to her credit, Diana struggled on, showing the strength she inherited from her strong-willed mother and her physically commanding father.

Underneath her frail exterior beat a heart of steel. And behind Diana's luminous eyes was a strength forged in the fires of adversity. She would need those gifts in the coming years.

One of her first duties was to decorate the newly-weds' private apartments at Kensington Palace. This task meant incorporating into their rooms the hundreds of wedding gifts received from well-wishers all around the world. It was a daunting task to mix and match gifts of various styles and taste, but Diana—with the help of a professional decorator—accomplished it.

Of course, Diana was keenly aware of her most important duty as the Princess of Wales. She was supposed to produce an heir. And she did. As she balanced her new duties and navigated a minefield of tradition and protocol, Diana one day revealed to her husband that she was pregnant.

Her condition was announced to the public in November 1981, and the news was greeted happily. But Diana's first Christmas as Princess proved to be miserable. She was suffering from daily bouts of morning sickness, as well as growing pains in her royal role.

A week later, on her first New Year's holiday with the royals, as Charles set out horseback riding, Diana had a terrible fall down a flight of steps. She was rushed to a doctor, where she and her baby were both pronounced in good health. But Diana had received injuries to her abdomen, and she was lucky that the accident didn't harm her or her unborn child.

In February, Charles and Diana flew to the Bahamas, where the Princess was secretly photographed wearing a bathing suit on a private beach. She was five months pregnant, and when the pictures were published in a British tabloid newspaper, Charles became very angry.

In June, Diana was rushed to the hospital. After a long and difficult labor, she gave birth to a son at 9:03 p.m. on June 21, 1982. The press promptly dubbed the child "Baby Wales" when the royal couple were slow to name the boy.

Charles favored the name Arthur, but Diana prevailed, and their first child was christened William. But to Diana, her beloved firstborn son would forever be "Will."

When the Queen came to visit her grandson, her first comment was, "Thank goodness he hasn't got ears like his father." Indeed, Will would come to resemble his beautiful mother more than his aristocratic father.

As Will grew older, Charles wanted him to be taken care of by a nanny. In this, too, Diana put her foot down. Recalling the endless succession of nannies who had raised her, Diana decided that she wanted to take care of the boy herself.

After the birth of Will, Diana seemed more

relaxed and contented. She fussed over her child, taking great care in every aspect of his nurturing.

Then, two months after the birth of William, tragedy struck. Princess Grace of Monaco, who had been so kind to Diana less than two years before, was killed in a car crash on a twisting stretch of road. Diana felt a kinship with the doomed Princess and insisted on going to her funeral. Charles had decided against her trip, but Diana had a strong will and was not to be deterred. She officially wrote the Queen a memo, requesting permission to go to the ceremony, which the Queen granted.

As one of her first solo acts as Princess of Wales, she attended Grace's lavish funeral in Monaco, and her performance impressed many in the royal family.

Diana also took Will, who was barely a toddler, on an extended state trip to Australia. It was the first time that a royal child had been carried across the world. In a nation of only 17 million people, more than a million Australians came out to greet the Prince and Princess. In Brisbane alone, over 300,000 people waited hours in 95-degree heat to catch a glimpse of the royal family and their young son.

Most of the press coverage of this trip focused on the Princess of Wales. Once again, Charles and the rest of the royals were astounded by Diana's popularity, both at home and abroad.

At first, Diana resented the bodyguards who followed her around day and night. But with time, she became friends with many of them. She was concerned with their personal problems, sent them birthday and Christmas greetings, and even letters of apology to their wives and children when the guards had to accompany her on long state visits. And Diana was deeply affected when one of her guards, Barry Mannakee, was killed in a motorcycle accident.

Diana's sincere concern for people whom others in the royal family usually took for granted further endeared her in the eyes of the common people.

When Diana was feeling blue, she often called her friend Sarah Ferguson, the daughter of Prince Charles's polo master. "Fergie," as she was called, would leave her job at a London art house to rush to Diana's side. And the Princess also enjoyed the company of her former roommate, Carolyn Bartholomew.

In 1984, Diana was pregnant again.

Charles wanted this child to be a girl, but Diana had already had tests performed and knew it was another son. She hid that fact from the Prince. When Harry was born, on September 15, the Prince openly expressed his disappointment.

"Oh, it's a boy," he remarked with mild disappointment. Then Prince Charles rushed off to play polo.

Chapter 10

Stiff Upper Lip

A breath of fresh air blew into Diana's life in June 1985, to help clear out some of the stuffy air of the royal court.

The Queen had contacted the Princess of Wales and asked for her advice. Her Majesty was having a bit of trouble assembling a guest list for the Royal Ascot race week celebrations.

"Could the Princess provide the names of any eligible single women to include in the festivities?" the Queen asked.

Diana immediately thought of her good friend Sarah Ferguson, and forwarded her name to the Queen's staff.

Although "Fergie" was single, she had been dating motor racing entrepreneur Paddy McNally for several months. But when the vivacious redhead received the royal invitation, she couldn't pass up the opportunity to see her friend Diana. Fergie arrived at Windsor Castle on a June afternoon in 1985, very excited.

A few hours later, at lunch, Sarah Ferguson

found herself seated next to Prince Charles's younger brother, Prince Andrew, the future Duke of York.

Andrew was nothing like his somber and serious brother, Prince Charles. For one thing, he was a full decade younger than the Prince. While Charles loved polo, fishing, and hunting, Andrew was content to stay at home and watch videos or cartoons on television. His biggest thrill was flying combat helicopters.

The future of the British monarchy did not rest on Andrew's head, so he tended to take life in stride, unlike his older, more serious brother.

Prince Andrew had chosen a career in the Royal Navy and was a combat veteran. During the Falklands Campaign of 1982, Andrew flew helicopters from the aircraft carrier HMS *Invincible*. His job was decoying Argentine Exocet missiles away from British ships, one of the most hazardous duties of the war.

Before his combat duty in the Falklands, Andrew had been dating an American actress. Their romance ended when the British press found out about it.

To almost everyone's surprise, when Prince Andrew met Sarah Ferguson, it was love at first sight. They stayed together for most of the day. Andrew tried to feed Fergie chocolates, and she laughingly refused.

Diana was too busy during that week of festivities to even notice the budding romance. Her royal duties still took up most of her time. When she found out about Fergie's new flame, she was as surprised as anyone.

By Christmas 1985, Andrew and Fergie were inseparable. In February 1986, Prince Andrew asked Sarah Ferguson to marry him.

She laughed out loud.

"When you wake up in the morning, you can tell me it was all a big joke," she replied.

But in the morning, Andrew asked her again. This time, Sarah accepted. A few days later, Prince Andrew and Sarah Ferguson announced their engagement to the world.

Although Fergie's popularity never approached Diana's, Andrew's fiancée was soon stalked by the media, too. Sarah's brash nature endeared her to the press and the royals.

Soon Diana had another "sister Sarah" to urge her into mischief. And, like two giggling school girls, the Princess and the Duchess did indeed get into trouble.

Their first great stunt was to try to crash Prince Andrew's bachelor party. Fergie and Diana disguised themselves as policewomen and approached the party, acting as if they were supposed to be there. But someone on the security staff recognized the famous pair, and they were turned away from the men-only affair.

The women then went to Annabel's, a fashionable nightclub in Berkeley Square, still in their police uniforms. They concluded the night by meeting Andrew's car when he returned home, still in uniform.

The stunt caused a mild scandal on the floor of Parliament, because impersonating a police officer was technically a crime. But the women's charade was greeted with amusement by most Britishers.

Compared with the novice Fergie, Diana performed at royal functions as if she had been born to the throne. Diana helped Fergie with her early public appearances and, after the wedding, with her royal duties as well.

Often when the two of them were together, their fun-loving natures took over and they got into mischief. But Diana didn't need Fergie around to cause a stir. She set high society buzzing all by herself when she decided to dance before the public in a surprise performance.

The incident occurred at the Royal Opera House, Covent Garden. The Princess of Wales and ballet star Wayne Sleep secretly choreographed a dance number to the Billy Joel song "Uptown Girl." The gala performance was viewed by Prince Charles and hundreds of aristocratic couples from all over Britain.

Near the end of the long charity show, Diana crept away from her husband and went backstage to change into a silver silk dress.

When the curtain rose again, there were gasps of

astonishment all over the opera house as the audience realized that the Princess of Wales was part of the entertainment.

In the end, the audience was so impressed that Diana took eight curtain calls. Charles declared that he was "amazed" by his wife's performance. He also disapproved. He felt it was undignified behavior for a future Queen.

Through it all, Diana got high marks as a mother. The press was impressed by the obvious affection she lavished on her two boys. And in a BBC interview taped at that time, she was seen romping with her boys on the floor of their nursery.

But Diana's duties still taxed her. The Princess didn't like to be away from her children for extended periods of time, but Charles didn't like his children traveling outside the country, either. So Diana, in order to fulfill her role as the future queen, often had to say good-bye to her two boys. She worried about them when she was not home, and this added to the burden of her responsibilities, and to her stress.

While she and Prince Charles were on an official trip to Canada, Diana grew quite weak. While the cameras were rolling, she put her arm on the shoulder of Prince Charles and whispered, "Darling, I think I am going to disappear." Then she fainted.

Against her doctor's wishes, Diana attended a state dinner that night and continued on with her trip, which ended in Japan. Diana looked pale and frail as she met representatives of the Japanese government, but she was determined to perform her royal duties to the best of her abilities.

Diana's continued antics with Sarah amused some of her subjects and shocked others. At a parade of young military officers at Sandhurst, Diana and Fergie were photographed poking their friend Lulu Blacker on the rump with their umbrellas. The British press soon dubbed Princess Diana and Sarah Ferguson "the Merry Wives of Windsor," but the nickname wasn't necessarily complimentary.

Many in the press thought the women acted too foolish for their station in society. But for others, Sarah and Diana's antics were a much-needed change from the stiff and formal royals.

Charles and Diana continued to have problems. Diana felt that Charles was too critical of her. Charles felt that Diana was sickly, unstable, and prone to dramatics. These factors, as well as their very different personalities, were putting a strain on the marriage.

Diana still battled with bulimia, and Charles, despite his wife's disapproval, continued his friendship with Camilla Parker-Bowles

But while Diana was on a ski trip in Switzerland, all thoughts of her own problems were pushed aside by the arrival of an unexpected visitor.

"There's been an accident," one of Prince Charles's valets said cryptically when he arrived at their chateau. Diana urged the man to tell her what was wrong, but he would not elaborate.

Finally, Diana and the pregnant Fergie learned that one of their dearest friends, Major Hugh Lindsay, had been killed in an avalanche. Even worse, he left behind a young wife who was several months pregnant.

Even Prince Charles was uncharacteristically distraught. In this crisis, it was Diana who pulled everyone together. She packed up the dead man's belongings, and convinced her husband that it was his duty to return to England with their friend's body.

To everyone's surprise, Diana took command of the situation. She even mothered her husband during his period of grief, much as she had mothered her own brother when he was growing up.

And when the Prince and Princess returned home, Diana took the man's widow by the hand and comforted her for days on end.

The tragedy was to have a profound effect on the young Princess. Diana learned she had the strength to deal with a crisis. And she discovered that she could help others in pain by being with them, taking them by the hand, and listening to their problems.

Diana learned that by offering others her love and compassion, she could make a difference in their lives.

It was a powerful and important lesson Diana would remember for the rest of her life.

❦❦ ─────────────────────────────────────

Chapter 11

New Beginnings

After the tragedy of Hugh Lindsay's death, Diana returned to England a changed woman. She seemed determined to take charge of her life, starting with her desire to control her bulimia. Toward that goal, she began to secretly read books on the subject, which she hid from her children, her husband, and even the servants, for fear that her problem would leak to the press.

She began to dabble in New Age philosophy and Eastern mysticism to better understand her disorder, and sought treatment in acupuncture.

She started to eat better and exercise more, with daily swims in Buckingham Palace and workouts at the London City Ballet or her favorite health club. She even learned *tai chi chuan*, a graceful exercise technique combining slow, deliberate martial arts movements with deep meditation.

Most of all, Diana tried to enjoy the simple pleasures of life more. Although she had always preferred light reading—she received personally autographed copies of each new novel from author

71

Danielle Steel—Diana began to also read books on philosophy and religion.

She continued to spend as much time as possible with her growing boys. She and Will grew especially close, and she continued to try to show her boys a side of the world that most royal children never get to see.

Part of her newfound control centered on her children's education. Diana firmly believed that her two sons should attend school with other children, while Charles favored private tutoring. In this, Diana prevailed, though both William and Harry do have a number of private teachers.

Charles also wanted his sons to attend the same boarding school as he had—Gordonstoun, a rigorous, isolated school on the northeastern coast of Scotland. But perhaps recalling the charming Eton graduates she had known as a teenager, or perhaps remembering Prince Charles's own stories of how he was bullied at Gordonstoun by the other boys, Diana insisted that William and Harry go first to Ludgrove school, then on to Eton.

In this, too, she prevailed.

Diana soon altered her physical appearance. She had her hair cut much shorter, and she became more confident and much livelier in public. She was now able to meet a stranger's gaze directly, and she managed the members of the press better, though she still resented the paparazzi, or photographers, stalking her and her sons.

Beginning in 1989, Diana moved beyond the polite charity balls of her peers and began true charitable work on her own, without the consent of the Queen. Her focus was on those unfortunate people whom society forgot, ignored, or shunned.

This phase of her life commenced when she was seen publicly hugging and holding the hands of AIDS victims. She wanted to show the world that these people were sick with a terrible disease, but that they should not be ostracized because of their illness.

She also began to make private visits to homeless shelters, as well as accompanying Roman Catholic Cardinal Basil Hume to a shelter for teenage runaways in London. There, many of the street children were hostile toward the Princess at first, but she soon won them over. Diana was perfectly at ease with these troubled young men and women.

When Prince Charles broke his arm in a polo match in 1990, Diana accompanied him to the hospital for a second operation to realign the broken bone. While she was there, Diana comforted the family of a man in a coma after a car crash. When the man recovered, Diana paid a private visit to him at his family home.

She also was able to help another family who had watched their mother die just moments before Diana arrived. The Princess heard the family sobbing and entered the woman's hospital room. The family, not knowing who she was, tolerated her presence because they thought she worked for the hospital.

Soon Diana was consoling the woman's husband and stepson on their loss. She later sent a handwritten note to the bereaved family.

Diana slowly increased her work with AIDS patients. She and First Lady Barbara Bush visited an AIDS shelter together in 1991. One of the patients burst into tears as Diana was speaking to him. She threw her arms around the distraught man and hugged him tightly. The sight profoundly affected all who were present that day.

Diana's brother Charles, now the Ninth Earl of Althorp, was also impressed with his sister's work with victims of AIDS.

"You have to be genuinely caring and able to give a lot of yourself to take on something other people wouldn't dream of touching," Charles Spencer told journalist Andrew Morton.

Diana came to believe that she no longer had to hide her true feelings—her true *self*—from the world. She began to more visibly strive to do good works and to be even more generous with her time, her energy, and her love.

"I reached a depth inside which I never imagined was possible," Diana told a friend. "My outlook on life has changed its course and become more positive and balanced."

Diana also strived constantly to instill those

qualities in her two sons. Her deepest wish was that Will would share her values so that when he ascended to the throne of England, he would be a very different kind of monarch than any who had come before.

Diana's hope was to modernize the monarchy and create a new kind of royal family, one more responsive to the needs and wishes of its subjects.

No one knows if she succeeded in this. Only time will tell.

Diana almost saw her hope for her nation's future vanish in 1991, when an accident nearly claimed the life of one of her children.

Diana was enjoying lunch with a friend when her bodyguard approached her. There had been an accident, he announced. William, the heir to the British throne, had suffered a severe head injury while playing with a golf club at Ludgrove school.

The Princess rushed to Will's side. While Diana and Prince Charles waited nervously, a CAT scan was performed on Prince William. Soon a neurosurgeon was consulted. Young Will, it was discovered, had suffered a depressed fracture of his skull. Surgery to relieve the pressure on the brain was immediately performed, which probably saved the young Prince's life.

But the danger had not passed. At any moment, Will's blood pressure could skyrocket—a common hazard after brain surgery that was nevertheless life-threatening.

Diana remained at Will's bedside all night, holding his hand and hoping and praying for a speedy recovery. Finally, doctors pronounced him out of danger.

A few days later, while Will was still mending at the hospital, Diana resumed her charity work in earnest. But as she visited a local charity hospital, a man in the crowd collapsed with a heart ailment. It was Diana who rushed to the man's aid, while cameras rolled and photos were snapped.

At the same time, Diana and Charles's tenth wedding anniversary was approaching. When a friend asked Diana what she had planned for the special occasion, she replied, "What is there to celebrate?"

This bitter statement perfectly summed up Diana's attitude to her marriage as she began her second decade as the Princess of Wales.

Royal Split

Just when it seemed that Diana's life, if not her marriage, was improving, tragedy struck again. While vacationing in Austria with her husband and sons, Diana was informed of her father's death. She prepared to depart for Kensington Palace, leaving Charles behind with Will and Harry.

To her surprise, the Prince of Wales insisted on accompanying his wife back to England. Diana demanded that Charles remain behind. She did not want her father's funeral to become a photo opportunity for her husband.

The two argued until the Princess told Charles that she would defer to the Queen's wishes. Her Majesty was called, and Charles accompanied Diana and the children back to England.

It was March 29, 1992. Diana and Charles had been drifting apart for several years.

Just two months before, the strain on the Prince and Princess was beginning to show. Word came to London that Mother Teresa had taken ill in Rome. Prince Charles insisted that flowers be sent to the woman who had dedicated her life to helping the poor in India.

But Diana didn't think flowers were enough. She jumped on a plane and flew to Rome to be at Mother Teresa's side.

Despite their marital problems, Diana continued to fulfill, and at times surpass, her role as Princess. When the Persian Gulf War began, Diana expressed a wish to visit the British troops serving in Saudi Arabia. The Palace felt that she would be too close to the danger of SCUD missile attacks. Diana instead visited Turkey and the families of some of the officers on the Iraqi front.

Her newfound confidence was sometimes surprising to others. Even as she attended official functions assigned to her by the Palace, Diana began to work for her own concerns. She took control of her schedule and began to open her own mail instead of relying on her ladies-in-waiting to screen it. AIDS hospices, homeless shelters, and food banks all benefitted from her charitable work.

In England, a man wrote to Diana telling her that his son, who was dying of AIDS, dearly wanted to meet the Princess. It was his final wish. Diana, upon reading the poignant letter, went to the dying man's side and spent time with him.

Though her good works were greeted with some skepticism by the British press, Diana had managed to impress some members of the royal family with her crusade. Even the Queen, who usually sided with her son in matters of state, was complimentary of Diana's charitable work.

For a brief time in March 1992, the media's attention was *not* focused on Diana. The Duke and Duchess of York had decided to separate.

Diana was sad to see Fergie's marriage crumble after only five years, but she was not surprised. Diana understood better than anyone how the glare of the media spotlight put a strain on a couple's personal life.

After Fergie's departure from the royal court, Diana became reflective about her role. She made a startling pronouncement to a family friend that would prove to be tragically prophetic. "I am performing a duty as the Princess of Wales as long as my time is allocated, but I don't see it any longer than fifteen years."

Diana died almost exactly fifteen years and one month after the title Princess of Wales was bestowed upon her.

Diana never allowed the press to invade the lives of her two sons. Nor did she allow the negative stories written about her or Prince Charles to affect their relationship with their sons.

Whenever possible, Diana brought her children along with her in her work. She was especially careful to do this with Will, because, like his father Prince Charles, Will is heir to Britain's throne—a future King.

Diana was determined that Will and Harry learn

about every facet of life, not just what goes on in the tiny, contained world of Buckingham Palace and the royal family. She took them shopping, to fast-food restaurants, to the movies—anywhere the boys could experience real life.

Diana also introduced them to her charity work. Once, when she visited a homeless shelter with Will, Diana got caught up in a conversation with the director of the charity. She soon realized that Will had gone off on his own. Diana found him playing chess with a homeless man, while others watched and cheered the boy on. It warmed her heart to see Will mix so well with people.

She knew then that she had instilled some of her own values and beliefs in the future monarch.

Will has been described as an intense, sensitive boy. His younger brother, Harry, is considered lively and mischievous—much like Diana as a child. But Will, especially, mimics some of his mother's mannerisms. He resembles her physically as well. Both Will and Harry are obviously Spencers—Harry even has the family's trademark rusty hair, just like Sarah, Diana's feisty older sister.

Diana had an easygoing relationship with her children. And they, in turn, felt protective toward her. Both Will and Harry saw their mother cry over the media hounding, and Will grew distrustful and shy around the press.

But at home, he was capable of some devilishness. A few years ago, as he and Diana were swimming in the outdoor pool at Highgrove, Diana left the water and changed into a dressing gown.

Will continued to splash about, until his mother ordered him out. Then Will began to thrash about in the deep water and cry out that he was drowning. He sank under the surface. Diana, in a panic, jumped into the water, dressing gown and all.

Will surfaced immediately, laughing and happily triumphant that he'd fooled "Mummy."

As the 1990s progressed, Diana continued to fulfill her duties as Princess with style and grace, as well as to find time for her charitable crusades. The work brought her much peace of mind.

"When I go home and turn my lights off at night, I know I did my best," she once said.

Diana did her best to save her marriage, too. But the task was hopeless. On December 9, 1992, she and Prince Charles announced their formal separation. The rift was front-page news all across the world.

"Buckingham Palace wrote the unhappy ending today to a storybook marriage gone badly wrong," the *New York Times* announced the next day.

"11 YEARS, 4 MONTHS, 1 WEEK, 4 DAYS," New York *Newsday*'s headline screamed, calculating how long the royal couple's marriage had lasted.

Charles was forty-four, Diana thirty-one.

In the separation and later divorce settlement, Diana was stripped of the honorific "Her Royal Majesty," but was permitted to retain the title

Princess of Wales. The couple continued to share custody of the children, and Diana remained in residence in Kensington Palace.

But the fairy tale had ended.

Now it was up to Diana to forge a new life for herself. A life without her Prince.

Chapter 13

ༀༀ

A New Beginning...A Sudden End

In August 1996, Diana's divorce from Prince Charles became final. Though the proceeding did not make Diana as independent as she felt when she first moved to London at the age of sixteen, she nevertheless felt more free than at any other time in her adult life. The divorce from Charles lifted a great weight off Diana's shoulders.

For the first time in over a decade, she was very much her own woman.

Shortly after their separation, in 1993, Diana had announced that she was cutting back on her charity work. But her sense of duty wouldn't allow her to do so for long. Soon she was back, giving speeches, raising money, and always finding time for those who were less fortunate.

In an interview on British television at this time, Diana said that she wanted to be "queen of people's hearts."

She said, "I think the biggest disease this world suffers from in this day and age is the disease of people feeling unloved, and I know that I can give love for a minute, for a half an hour, for a day, for a month. But I can give, and I'm very happy to do that, and I want to do that."

In that same interview, Diana evaded the question of whether or not Charles should be crowned King, but it seemed obvious that she believed her son Will to be better qualified for the title.

Indeed, Diana lavished even more time and attention on her children after her separation and divorce. And sometimes, she played the role of Supermom, fulfilling the dreams of her two sons.

When Diana learned that young Will had a crush on Cindy Crawford, she invited the supermodel to tea at Kensington Palace. Ms. Crawford was ushered into a private room, where she found Will waiting for her. The youth spoke to the model for a few minutes, blushing constantly. A short time later, Diana arrived for tea and introductions.

And it was Diana who planned a dream vacation for her two boys in the United States. She entered the country with her two children secretly, and went to stay at a ranch belonging to Goldie Hawn and Kurt Russell. While there, Diana and the boys drove four-wheel-drive recreational vehicles, rode horses, and went whitewater rafting.

Diana accompanied her boys to water parks, movies, the theater, concerts, and amusement parks. She was determined to be available to her children, and to give them the love, support, and time that she had longed for as a child.

She also consciously sought to emulate Mother Teresa. At a cancer ward in Pakistan, Diana held a dying baby in her arms. The child had an ugly festering wound on its face that smelled bad. Like Mother Teresa, Diana ignored her own discomfort and cradled the child in her lap for hours.

When she learned that the baby had died a few days later, Diana was so upset that she couldn't speak.

Diana soon found new causes to champion. One of her crusades was particularly controversial. When Diana heard about the pain and destruction caused by land mines—bombs buried in the ground by the military during times of war—she became an active opponent of the use of such weapons.

She went to Angola to see firsthand the wounds inflicted by these weapons on innocent people who unwittingly detonated the hidden devices.

Her work with AIDS patients, cancer patients, and the poor continued unabated after the divorce.

The year 1997 was a busy one for the Princess, and she seemed to sense that her future was uncertain.

Publicly, Diana was able to joke with Barbara Walters about dating again, about the lack of eligible bachelors, and about her controversial divorce and new relationship with the royals.

Privately, she was very lonely. Both of her boys were off in boarding school at Eton for most of the year, and Diana had only her charity work and her duties as Princess to relieve her solitude. She felt very much like an isolated princess trapped in an ivory tower of title and celebrity.

But Diana was to find some comfort from an unlikely source. In 1997, she began to date a man named Dodi Al Fayed, the son of an Egyptian-born millionaire. Dodi's father, Mohamed Al Fayed, owned the London department store Harrods and had been a close friend of Diana's father. In fact, Johnnie Spencer had asked Mohamed to watch over his daughter shortly before his death in 1992.

In July 1997, Dodi and Diana were photographed together at St. Tropez in France. Along with Diana were her two sons. The vacation was a nice respite for Diana, and she regretted that she had to return to London on July 21.

But within hours of her arrival at Kensington Palace, Diana was told of the murder of her friend, fashion designer Gianni Versace, in Miami. Diana immediately flew to Milan, Italy, for Versace's funeral. During the service, Diana was seated next to a distraught Elton John. She consoled the tearful singer during the funeral and afterward.

In August, Diana traveled to war-torn Bosnia as part of her crusade against land mines. She met with children and adults who had been injured by the deadly weapons. Afterward, she returned to England and paid a visit to her favorite psychic, Rita Rogers. She brought Dodi along, and the couple flew on his private helicopter to Derbyshire for the meeting. Diana seemed to have found happiness.

But she may have been hesitant to wed so soon after her divorce. Diana told a British society columnist: "I haven't taken such a long time getting out of one poor marriage to get into another."

On August 21, Diana departed with Dodi for a cruise of the Mediterranean on the Al Fayed family yacht. The couple then flew to Paris, where they arrived on Saturday, August 30, 1997.

That night, Dodi and Diana planned to have a quiet dinner at a restaurant at Dodi's father's hotel, the Paris Ritz. But when the couple entered the dining room, they felt the eyes of everyone on them, so they retired to a private room to enjoy their meal in peace.

Dodi had purchased an elegant $205,000 ring for Diana and written a poem for her that he had engraved on a plaque and placed under her pillow. Speculation was that the young Egyptian millionaire was going to ask Diana to marry him that night.

When their dinner was over, Dodi called for the head of hotel security, Henri Paul. Together, they hatched a scheme to dodge the paparazzi.

Dodi's regular driver took Dodi's personal limousine and drove away from the Ritz, hoping to lure some of the photographers away. The plan didn't work as well as hoped. When Diana and Dodi— along with driver Henri Paul and Dodi's bodyguard

Trevor Rees-Jones—left the hotel in a Mecerdes S-280, the paparazzi were right behind them on motorcycles.

The Mercedes was driving at a high speed. The photographers were in full pursuit. Only Rees-Jones wore a seat belt. We may never know exactly what happened. But in a tunnel under a Paris boulevard, driver Henri Paul lost control of the speeding vehicle.

The limousine crashed into a road divider, skidded across the highway, and bounced off the walls of the tunnel. The car flipped over once before landing upright on its wheels.

The driver and Dodi Al Fayed were killed instantly.

The bodyguard and the Princess, still alive, were trapped in the wreckage. As photographers snapped pictures of the Mercedes, and its gravely injured passengers, French emergency crews arrived. It took them two hours to free Diana from the car.

At the hospital, doctors worked frantically to save the Princess's life. But it was no use. The injuries were massive, and in the hours it took to free Diana, she had lost a lot of blood. Doctors massaged her heart for over an hour to keep it beating.

But as strong as she was in life, even Diana could not cheat death. The Princess of Wales was pronounced dead early Sunday morning.

At Balmoral Castle, where William and Harry were vacationing with their father, the boys were awakened at dawn by Prince Charles and told of their mother's death.

The world awoke that Sunday morning to the unbelievable news. The fairy tale life of Diana Spencer had ended.

Chapter 14

"*Good-bye, England's Rose*"

In the days following Diana's sudden, tragic death, a spontaneous outpouring of grief was expressed all over the world. The terrible sense of shock was soon replaced by one of loss, a loss felt most keenly by her children and family, but also the millions of people who had come to know her.

Flowers were placed in her honor in front of Kensington and Buckingham palaces—so many flowers that there were none left in all of Great Britain by the Monday following her death. Frantic florists had to import flowers from Holland.

By the day of her funeral, it was estimated that over a million flowers had been laid in front of Diana's former home at Kensington Palace.

Diana's funeral was to take place on the Saturday following her death. It was not to be a state funeral. Because of the divorce, Diana was no longer entitled to one. But anyone who watched the ceremony on that sunny Saturday afternoon could not possibly tell the difference.

Heads of state, religious leaders, celebrities, and members of Diana's many charitable organizations were invited to the emotional service at Westminster Abbey in the heart of London.

For the first few days after her death, Diana's sons remained at Balmoral Castle, consumed by grief and incomprehension. On the day they learned of their mother's death, they made a brief public appearance to attend church services with their father. The boys spoke to mourners and gazed at the spontaneously constructed shrine of cards and flowers that grew in front of the castle's main gate.

William looked composed, but his eyes avoided the cameras. Harry seemed in control, but there was a haunted look of bewilderment on his young face.

As the grim week of mourning passed with no statement from Queen Elizabeth II, the people of Great Britain began to ask questions.

Where is our Queen? Why is she not sharing her grief with us?

Finally, on the day before Diana's funeral, the seventy-one-year-old monarch appeared on live television to give a special address to the nation. It was only the second time in her forty-year reign that Elizabeth II had gone before her subjects in this fashion.

Her decision to appear was unprecedented—a sign that the royals were bending to their bereaved subjects' hopes and wishes. This was something

Diana had wanted to see happen ever since she'd entered the royal family.

In an emotional statement, the Queen acknowledged "the extraordinary and moving reaction to [Diana's] death" and said that the Princess "never lost her capacity to smile and laugh, nor inspire others with her warmth and kindness."

"We have all been trying in our different ways to cope," the Queen continued. "It is not easy to express a sense of loss since the initial shock is often succeeded by a mixture of other feelings: disbelief, incomprehension, anger—and concern for those who remain."

All of those emotions were experienced by the British people that week. Feelings of disbelief and incomprehension were especially powerful, as were feelings of concern for Diana's two sons.

It was as if the world had suddenly discovered how special Diana truly was. And, in that discovery, the world began to understand how very much it would miss her presence.

Diana's brother, Charles, Earl of Althorp, expressed anger at her death. In a statement shortly after the accident, he lashed out at the paparazzi who had stalked his sister since her marriage to Prince Charles.

"I always believed that the press would kill her in the end," he said. "But not even I believed they would take such a direct hand in her death."

As the grim week progressed, the world was

shaken by another tragedy. Mother Teresa was dead. Only a few months before, Diana had met with the sister at a shelter in New York City. The two spoke at length and had their picture taken by dozens of photographers as they laughed, talked, and smiled.

And now, both of these remarkable women were gone forever.

As more than a million people filed into London, the distance Diana's funeral procession would travel was lengthened to accommodate all of the mourners. Soon it was announced that Elton John, one of Diana's favorite performers, would sing a song dedicated to the memory of the late Princess.

With the help of Bernie Taupin, Elton John rewrote the lyrics to one of his most popular songs, "Candle in the Wind." It was a song originally written in remembrance of the actress Marilyn Monroe, who'd died tragically at the same young age as Diana.

As Elton John sang at Diana's funeral, people outside the church lit candles and cradled them in their hands. His poignant and heartfelt performance moved almost everyone to tears.

Many people spoke at the funeral, expressing their profound grief at Diana's passing. Her sister Sarah, Prime Minister Tony Blair, and the Archbishop of Canterbury were but a few. But the most powerful and sincere message of them all was delivered by her grieving younger brother, Charles.

He acknowledged his sister's human frailties

and insisted that there was no need to "canonize" her, or think of her as a saint. Diana, he said, was "someone with a natural nobility who was classless, who proved in the last year that she needed no royal title to continue to generate her particular brand of magic."

When the Earl of Althorp stepped from the podium, spontaneous applause could be heard from the crowd outside the cathedral. Soon a wave of applause moved through the solemn mourners inside Westminster Abbey as well.

A million people lined the route of the funeral procession. As Diana's coffin passed, hundreds of thousands of flowers were tossed onto the hearse. The driver had to stop intermittently to clear the windshield so he could see.

Diana's body was laid to rest in a final, private ceremony. She was buried on a tiny island in the middle of a lake on her family's ancestral estate, Althorp.

Her funeral was the most watched event in television history. Over two and a half *billion* people tuned in as Diana, the Princess of Wales, was laid to rest.

But she will never be forgotten. Her star will never dim. In the end, Diana became what she'd set out to become—an inspiration to the people of the world, an example of selfless work and boundless love.

Our Queen of Hearts.